CHOCOLATE

The Connoisseur's
Companion

CHOCOLATE

*The Connoisseur's
Companion*

Cover: 15th-century miniature,
Lombard school, from an ancient codex.

First published in Great Britain in 1999 by
PAVILION BOOKS LIMITED
London House, Great Eastern Wharf
Parkgate Road, London SW11 4NQ

Copyright © 1995 Nardini Editore, Fiesole (FI), Italy
Text by Marco Menabuoni
English translation © Pavilion Books Limited 1999

A CIP catalogue record for this book is available
from the British Library.

ISBN 1 86205 339 1

Set in Times New Roman
Printed in Italy

2 4 6 8 10 9 7 5 3 1

This book can be ordered direct from the publisher.
Please contact the Marketing Department.
But try your bookshop first.

CHOCOLATE

The marvel of a steaming-hot drink

When it is cold or when it is damp and foggy, and indeed whenever we feel tired and depressed, there is nothing more reviving or uplifting for the spirits than a delicious cup of hot, steaming chocolate. No one would deny

that a cup of hot chocolate encourages friendship, goodwill and possibly even love.

We do not mean by this that a cup of hot chocolate is necessarily an aphrodisiac, but there is no doubt that it puts fire and vigour in the veins, making people good humoured and well disposed towards one another. Cocoa, chocolates and those wonderful brown bars of chocolate that we turn to for comfort when we are depressed: in all its forms, chocolate is a gift of nature as remarkable as coffee. It is a "wonderful" substance which supports one on the difficult journey through adversity. Throughout history sensible people have drawn strength from it like thirsty travellers from healthy spring water.

There was a time when cocoa powder mixed with spices and diluted in hot water was, not without reason, seen as a "divine" beverage because of its miraculous qualities. It was a gift of the gods, something that man had discovered but which had always remained concealed, almost as if to hide its restorative powers. For a long time cocoa also had a ritual significance as well as a medicinal one, and at court the habit of drinking a cup of hot chocolate was considered a sign of distinction and nobility.

With this long tradition it is evident that the delights of cocoa and chocolate

yliyocan.

have appealed not just to children and gourmets, but to everyone who enjoys a beverage which is as uplifting as it is delicious.

An ancient legend

Montezuma was the emperor of the Aztecs at the time when Mexico was conquered by the Spaniards under the leadership of Hernán Cortés. The peoples of his empire included the Aztecs themselves, the Olmecs, the Toltecs and the Mayas. Since time immemorial these peoples had been familiar with a striking native tree with large, horizontal branches which in turn produced smaller boughs. This was the cacao or cocoa tree. Its branches grow leaves at various times of the year depending on rainfall, with colours ranging from pink

13

to dark violet and green. The twin-jointed leaf stalks enable the leaves always to be turned towards the light. The flowers are white and pink and flower all year round. They are hermaphrodite, with both male and female reproductive organs.

The valleys round Tenochtitlán (where Mexico City is today) were always covered with flowers and the Spanish were quite awed by this breathtaking spectacle.

The flowers are pollinated by small insects, but on average only one flower in 500 develops into a fruit, the cocoa pod. This is very like papaya or quince in shape, and it contains the cocoa beans. The outside covering has furrows which harden as the fruit matures.

The Mexicans told the Spanish that the tree had an average lifespan of forty years and that the yield varied very much from year to year. The bishop and chronicler Diego de Landa wrote that "Cocoa is the gold of this country and it is even used as money at the market in Chichén Itza" (a religious centre). Merchants selling cocoa beans were highly respected and exempt from tax, while an imperial decree ordered each farmer to devote at least 400 square feet (nearly 40 square metres) to the cultivation of the cocoa tree.

Aztec cooks were extremely sophisticated and they used a wide range of ingredients such as flour, eggs and sugar to make tarts, biscuits and cakes, to the great delight of the emperor and his courtiers. But although he loved all this delicious food, what Montezuma enjoyed more than anything was *chocolátl*, a tasty cocktail prepared from cocoa powder, vanilla and other spices. According to chroniclers of the period, the divine emperor drank at

Cioacoatl.

Capitulo ſexto, ſo ibidem.

least forty cups of it a day! Montezuma never used the same cup twice: as soon as the meal was finished, the crockery used for the royal repast was given away to some nobleman of the court who was highly honoured to use the plates and cups his emperor had touched.

Why were the Aztecs so keen on this drink? It is said to be because of an ancient legend, which went as follows. Once upon a time there was a very beautiful princess whose husband went

16

to war in a distant land, leaving her in charge of an enormous treasure. The princess was besieged by enemies who wanted to lay their hands on the treasure. When she was captured she refused to reveal where the treasure was hidden. Her enemies were furious and killed her. According to this ancient legend the cocoa tree grew from her blood, and that is why its beans are as bitter as her suffering, as red as her blood, and as stimulating and strong as her virtue.

Varieties

According to the classification used in Latin America today, there are three types of cocoa: *criollo*, *forastero* and *trinitario*.

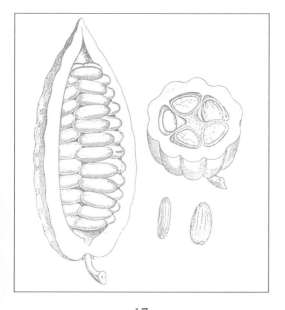

The name of the first type means "indigenous" or "native" in South American Spanish and it is the name given to the cocoa of the Aztecs by the country's first discoverers. The bean pods of this variety of cocoa tree are elongated and grooved, green when they first develop and becoming reddish-orange when they ripen. The beans themselves are whitish and matt. This kind of cocoa tree is mainly cultivated in Mexico, Venezuela, Colombia and a few places in Asia. In spite of the quality and pleasant taste of the cocoa powder made from its beans, it is being cultivated less and less because the yield is low and it is prone to disease.

The name *forastero* ("strange" or "exotic") was given by people of Central America to the cocoa plant originally from the upper basin of the River Amazon in Brazil. The pod is roundish, rather smooth, greenish when it first develops and turning a brilliant yellow when the fruit is ripe. The cocoa known as *forastero* includes the best production in Brazil, the *nacional* grown in Ecuador, and various species cultivated in other Latin American countries, in Java and in Sri Lanka.

The *trinitario* species is very different. It may have originated from cross-fertilisation between the *criollo* from Trinidad and the *forastero*. However that may be, today the *trinitario* variety is very widespread and it forms a homogenous group. Its pods have a characteristic violet colour and produce an excellent cocoa, rather similar in taste and quality to *forastero*.

From the tree to the cup

A member of the *Sterculiaceae* family, the cocoa tree was given its scientific name *Theobroma cacao* by the famous Swedish naturalist Carl von Linné, commonly known as Linnaeus. The first name came from the Greek words meaning "food of the gods", while the second word is derived from the Aztec

Linnaeus

name for the cocoa plant, *cacahuátl*. It seemed to be a native of tropical America and therefore needed a hot and humid climate.

Hernán Cortés

It was Hernán Cortés, the Spanish conqueror of Montezuma's empire, who first introduced cocoa beans into Europe in the mid-16th century. Until then, both cocoa and chocolate, which is derived from it, were completely unknown in the West.

The plant which produces these valuable beans is a very deep-rooted tree, six to eight metres (20 to 25 feet) high, which is kept low by frequent pruning. It does not need a lot of light but it dislikes excessive temperature variation. That is why it was protected on the high Mexican plateaus – as it still is today – by other taller, more robust trees, which shielded the cocoa tree from strong winds and sun. This shading technique was called *sombreamento*, a term still used today. After being in contact with the Spanish, the Mexicans called the fruit *cabosse*, a word which today refers to harvest time when the fruit changes colour, from reddish-green to orange-red.

Writers at the time of the Conquest of Mexico noted that the leaves of the plant were alternate, that the green or red flowers appeared directly on the trunk and old branches, that the fruits were oval-shaped pods up to 15 cm (6 in) long, containing about 40 beans, arranged in rows of 5. These beans

Montezuma

were then left to ferment, drying in the sun or piled up in pits or open baskets. Today cocoa beans are sold in sacks of about 80 kg (175 lb).

Depending on where the product comes from, cocoa beans are divided as follows:

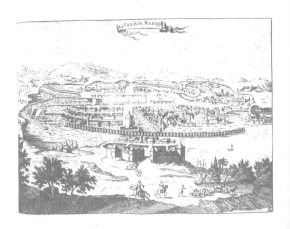

American cocoa: the most valued is Mexican cocoa but it is also cultivated in Venezuela, Columbia, Guatemala and Ecuador; the Bahia variety grown in Brazil is also much sought after.

Asian cocoa: this is produced in Sri Lanka and Java.

African cocoa: the Akka type grown in Ghana is highly regarded, but the varieties cultivated in Cameroon and Madagascar are also important.

Although intensively cultivated in Mexico at the time of the Spanish Conquest, the cocoa tree is probably native to the Amazon River basin and the Brazilian tropical rainforest. The Indians already knew about grinding the beans to produce what is variously known in Europe as "chocolate", "cioccolata", "chocolate" (Spanish, pronounced "choco-la-tay"), "Schokolade", "chocolat", and similar sounding words.

The pre-Colombian tribes of Mexico and Central America mixed the powder obtained by grinding the beans with maize flour, to which they added a little hot water, thus producing a thick paste.

The Spanish conquerors of Mexico soon learned to appreciate this dark beverage which seemed to give unexpected strength and energy. A chroni-

cler of the period wrote that "if the Indians were deprived of this drink they felt less well, and I myself experienced this when I was in Mexico because I drank this chocolate drink and I liked it a lot and it made me feel really good and I felt I could not spend a day without drinking some […]".

Today it is known that the euphoria produced by chocolate can be scientifically explained. As well as water, nitrogenous substances, starch, sugars, fats, tannins and cellulose, cocoa (like coffee and tea) contains an alkaloid of the purine group which has a psycho-analeptic effect on those who consume it. Cocoa contains large amounts of teobromine which stimulates the central nervous system, and has diuretic and vaso-dilating properties. The beneficial effects naturally depend on the quantity absorbed, although it is known that Voltaire drank no fewer than a dozen cups of chocolate a day, and that Napoleon turned to what he called the "brown drink" when he felt mentally exhausted.

Cocoa also contains phosphorus: 625 mg per 100 g of cocoa, much more than fish, which averages 240 mg per 100 g. It is also rich in iron (14 mg per 100 g), calcium, magnesium and other vitamins. Cocoa beans have about 50 per cent of various fats, one of which is cocoa butter. This pleasantly flavoured yellowish-white substance consists of esters of oleic and palmitic acids. Besides being used to make chocolate, cocoa butter is also used in the pharmaceutical industry as an inert bulking agent in ointments, suppositories and

the like, and in cosmetic creams and lipsticks.

Hot chocolate is a balanced food, containing 35 per cent vegetable fats, 16 per cent proteins and 23 per cent carbohydrates. It is one of the basic nutrients prescribed by NASA scientists for the diet of astronauts.

It is also a useful addition to the diet of an energetic adult. A man of average size, weighing about 70 kg (11 stone), should have a daily intake of about 2,500 calories. If he works out or does any demanding sport he will need about 5,000 calories. Given that a cup of chocolate or a bar of chocolate have a much higher calorie content than, for instance, bread or veal, and that teobromine has stimulating and fortifying properties, it is easy to understand why chocolate is so popular among sports people when they need a quick, effective boost of energy.

It has been mentioned that hot chocolate may cause digestive problems. But it should be pointed out that chocolate remains in the stomach for under 2 hours, while wholemeal bread remains 3 hours and a steak or boiled haricot beans stay at least 4 hours.

Adulteration

One of the most important elements which make chocolate such a nutritious food for all ages, appreciated by an ever-increasing number of people, is undoubtedly the quality of the cocoa. The cocoa used to make chocolate, whether at a craft level or industrially, must be absolutely pure, without any adulteration.

Any of the shortcomings or drawbacks attributed to chocolate are often caused by some kind of adulteration. One should be not be tempted by cheap, anonymous products which are more likely to be adulterated. It is true that genuine products cost a little more but the price is a guarantee of authenticity.

Sisarum Peruvianum, sine Batata Hispanorum.
Potatus, or Potato's.

Adulteration sometimes takes place in the country where the cocoa has been produced: cocoa is very easy to tamper with. One of the commonest frauds is the addition of fats, such as fish oil, palm oil, margarine or paraffin. The weight of cocoa can also be artificially increased by adding the residue of the ground cocoa beans to the original cocoa powder, or mixing it with potato flour, whale oil or extra sugar.

This type of adulteration is serious commercial fraud, and indeed adulteration is punishable by law in all countries. But the only way to avoid falling victim to this sort of swindle is to buy good-quality products marketed by well-established manufacturers, and to check the label for provenance. Where any substitute is used this should be mentioned clearly on the label, although the word "substitute" often appears in very small print which is almost impossible to read, in the hope of escaping attention and misleading the consumer.

CULTIVATION
AND HARVESTING

Notes on production

It has already been mentioned that the cultivation and production of cocoa spread from Central America to Africa and Asia, naturally always in tropical climate zones with a hot and humid climate. Now Latin America's production has been overtaken by Africa, or rather some countries in Africa. The result is that the country which produces the most cocoa in absolute terms is the Ivory Coast with almost 720,000 tons of beans per year, followed by Brazil, Ghana and Malaysia.

For some years the major cocoa-producing countries have been trying to reach agreement about tailoring their own production to demand, and above all to maintain prices at recent levels after a period of overproduction which caused prices to tumble. But in 1993 the harvest was bad everywhere which naturally led to a rise in prices.

The commitment of farmers has to be fairly long-term since the cocoa tree only reaches productive maturity after eight years, then continuing to produce for several decades. Quality has been improved by grafting which has led to new varieties. A hectare of cultivated land produces approximately 500 kg of cocoa beans (about 200 lb per acre).

Harvesting the fruit

When the fruit is ripe and has changed colour it is harvested, using a sharp machete. The pod containing the beans is easier to remove when the fruit is ripe.

In ancient times the beans were left to ferment after being harvested, but normally this no longer takes place. The beans are cleaned and carefully selected, with some samples being taken. They are then put in sacks and sent to the various processing factories. Once they have arrived there, the sacks are emptied and the beans are carried to various storage silos by conveyor belts, depending on their country of origin; this is because the person in charge of blending must know precisely where the beans come from. Naturally, every manufacturer tries to obtain

a blend whose taste is superior to that produced by the others. To achieve this, the various kinds of cocoa are

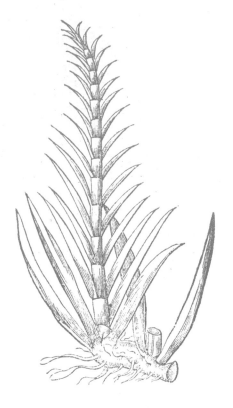

Arundo Saccharina.
Sugar Cane.

mixed according to pre-determined for-
mulae using recorded proportions and
quantities to obtain the desired blend.
The beans are then released into ovens
where they are roasted at 130° C (about
265° F) and then dried at roughly 80° C
(175° F) in order to preserve the aroma
better.

If the pod does not easily detach
itself from the fruit, a machine first
breaks open the covering and separates

it from the fruit inside (the so-called "almond"), which is then left to ferment in a hot, humid atmosphere, having first been sprinkled with an alkaline carbonate solution.

Next, the "almonds" are ground in a mill with rotating discs which reduce the beans to a semi-liquid paste, or chocolate liquor. The cocoa butter (which forms about 50 per cent of the total) melts as a result of the heat produced by the rotating discs.

The chocolate liquor is then used to make cocoa powder. First much of the cocoa butter is extracted using hydraulic presses. Then the substance that remains is ground more to obtain an even finer result. Sugar is added (in the preparation of sweet chocolate) and the mixture is further refined in machines with multiple cylinders. The refining process takes place in containers heated to about 80° C (175° F) in which the mixture is slowly stirred for a period defined by how fine a paste is required for chocolate. During the refining process, the saccharose is converted into levulose as a result of a chemical process known as hydrolysis: this plays a particularly important part in the preparation of plain chocolate paste, giving it its characteristic flavour.

Once the refining process is completed, the paste is placed in special vessels where, still hot, it is subjected to a continuous rotating movement for approximately 48 hours. This serves to amalgamate the components while simultaneously removing any unpleasant acidity.

It is during this phase of the production, the "flavouring" of the chocolate, that other substances may be added to the product such as soya lecithin or vanilla. For milk chocolate, condensed milk is added to the paste.

When the 48 hours in the rotating vessel are completed, the chocolate is ready to be moulded according to the requirements of the manufacturer who naturally aims to satisfy his customers'

taste. The molten chocolate paste is poured into special moulds. These filled moulds are then placed on vibrating surfaces so that any air bubbles still present in the paste will come to the surface and burst. Finally, the moulds are put in refrigerators to cool down.

Diseases

One of the commonest diseases leading to the premature death of the cocoa tree is a rot attacking its roots which is caused by a fungus of the basidio-mycete class. These fungi reproduce fairly slowly, so a grower who becomes aware of the fungus can protect the trees not yet infected by the parasite by creating a safety zone separating them from the diseased ones. The latter must then be cut down: a terrible sacrifice, but one which has to be made.

Another disease affecting cocoa trees is tracheomycosis, another fungal disease, which attacks the top of the tree, blocking the lymphatic vessels where the vital sap is situated and causing its death in a very short time. In this case too there is no fungicide capable of combating the disease and the grower is forced to cut down the affected tree.

Yet another mycotic or fungal disease is caused by *Verticillium dahliae*, a class of imperfect fungus which also causes tracheomycosis, but this time preventing the vital sap from travelling to the roots, thus causing the leaves and flowers to fall, and making the development of fruit impossible.

The fruit itself can be attacked by

moniliasis (a disease which also affects man, attacking the mucous membranes). However, this only exists in a few Latin American countries and not at all in Africa or elsewhere. Recent studies have pointed to the fact that the disease thrives on excessively damp soil caused by intense tropical rains. When a cocoa tree is affected by moniliasis the first symptom is that the pod starts displaying dark spots; it is then covered by white mycelium (the "cells" of the fungi) which produce spores, capable of reproducing themselves.

A tree affected by moniliasis may lose up to 15 per cent of its yield. The disease is carried from plant to plant by an insect of the *Homoptera* order, equipped with special mouth parts suitable for pricking and sucking. The spread of this disease varies from region to region because the disease-carrying insects fly from tree to tree if the soil is clean and carefully weeded, but if they find some suitable undergrowth they will travel from plant to plant on the ground.

Once affected, all the farmer can do is to create isolation zones round the diseased trees so that the healthy trees are protected. To do this, he must cut the sick trees down and create a void around the healthy ones. Fortunately, there are good fungicides and insecticides which at least in part combat this disease.

Today, agronomists and farmers pay particular attention to choosing and preparing the region and soil earmarked for the planting of trees for cocoa production. Thus, clear streams will often be found running near plantations of cocoa trees, and thickets of other trees are frequently planted to shade the cocoa trees from the direct rays of the sun.

THE SPREAD
OF CHOCOLATE

The drink of kings

The first European to have discovered cocoa was most probably Christopher Columbus. During his voyages of discovery he will have been able to see cocoa trees and witness the ritual – as it was then considered – of the "caciques" (the indigenous local chiefs) who drank the powder of the beans of this plant mixed with hot water. But Columbus did not like the taste, nor did he realise the commercial importance of the product.

The introduction of cacao or cocoa to Spain and from there to the rest of Europe was due, as has already been mentioned, to the conquistador Hernán Cortés who had tasted it at the court of Montezuma. The importance which Central American people attached to this chocolate drink is well illustrated by a custom which the conquistadors found surprising. The Mayas never had

more than one wife each, but she could be divorced if it turned out that she was sterile or if she forgot to prepare the daily steam bath for her husband according to the rules. Caught in such a predicament – and the same applied if she was caught in the act of adultery – the woman would be tried. In his judgement the village chief would declare that because of her guilt she would no longer be able to "drink chocolate in the shade of the first tree in the world", a great dishonour.

The daily ritual of the "cup of chocolate" was practised by the whole population of Mexico, from Montezuma down to the lowest subject in the empire during the first half of 16th century. The Spanish invaders attending the ceremony were so struck by it that they decided to introduce the beans into Europe. They had noticed that the powder obtained by grinding the cocoa beans, dissolved in water and mixed with spices, produced a certain euphoria, a feeling of well-being, and helped to supply the energy needed to carry out the tasks of the day.

It was Charles V who ruled over the new American colonies where this plant was grown, and at his court the beans were roasted and ground, dissolved in hot water, sweetened with honey and whipped with a stick to make a beautiful foamy head; the

CARLO V.

Spanish nobles often also added a beaten egg yolk to their chocolate drink.

But what is even more interesting is how a cup of steaming hot chocolate became a real ceremony – or rather remained one, since the ritual had been practised for centuries by the Aztecs. The nobles or hidalgos and other aristocrats sipped their hot chocolate while the court musicians played romantic tunes and gypsy dancers performed their wild art.

From Spain and the Spanish court, chocolate soon spread all over Europe, and more especially to the French court. It is remarkable how quickly this completely unknown beverage spread with such rapidity.

Chocolate in Europe

After the fortuitous and fortunate discovery of the cocoa tree and the use the Indians made of the ground beans, the Spanish started selling cocoa paste prepared in the colonies all over Europe. But the very high prices restricted the consumption of cocoa to the royal courts and the rich aristocracy.

Nevertheless, the new beverage became extremely popular, partly as a result of the visits of important officials to the Spanish court, its success among prelates and monks, and through the

Anne of Austria

trading of cocoa by pirates who seized the ships returning from Mexico.

Cocoa as a drink was officially introduced at the French court when Anne of Austria, daughter of King Philip III of Spain, married Louis XIII. It is said that with the rest of her luggage the new sovereign brought with her everything that was necessary to make hot chocolate. It could be prepared single-handedly by her favourite maid-in-waiting at court. When fifty years later, Louis XIV, the Sun King, married Maria Theresa, the Spanish Infanta, she introduced the custom of drinking a cup of hot chocolate on waking up and during audiences. This

Cardinal Mazarin

made the drink which had come all the way from the New World even more popular.

At the end of the 16th century there were at least twenty different recipes for the preparation of hot chocolate. But it was no simple task: experts were needed to perform it, and this is why the queens of France who had come from Spain had been accompanied by "chocolate makers", chambermaids and manservants whose only task was to prepare this highly fashionable drink.

It is also known that Cardinal Mazarin was a great consumer o chocolate, as his famous predecessor, Cardinal Richelieu had been. He went so far as to say that chocolate was a miraculous drink, an infallible panacea against every disease.

Mazarin himself had his own cook whose task it was to have a cup of steaming hot chocolate ready for his master whenever he felt like having one. The Sun King even granted a "patent" or "monopoly" to an official of the Queen's Guard to sell and prepare cocoa powder throughout the country: this happened in 1659 and the patent was valid for thirty years.

At the University of Paris in 1664, a certain François Foucault who was

studying there graduated in medicine with a thesis on chocolate, which was described as an energy-giving food and also as an excellent remedy for bilious problems.

But there were some who disagreed. For instance, Madame de Sévigné – a French writer of the second half of the 17th century – sent a famous letter to

her daughter to warn her against the excessive consumption of chocolate. She referred to one of her acquaintances who, having drunk too much chocolate during pregnancy, gave birth to a son with black skin who died a few hours later.

Meanwhile the cultivation of the cocoa tree was spreading to the islands of the Caribbean as a result of the British starting to cultivate it in Martinique and Jamaica.

Then the Dutch succeeded in taking over the cocoa trade, thus becoming the greatest cocoa traders in the world. As excellent seafarers, they succeeded in seizing the monopoly on the cocoa trade from the Spanish by using a cunning stratagem. The King of Spain had granted the British the exclusive right to supply black slaves to the colonies across the Atlantic. This was valid for thirty years. In order to get round this, the Dutch captured negroes in Africa and exchanged them for the precious cocoa beans in America. Being paid neither in gold nor silver they did not infringe the royal edict.

Cocoa was always eagerly awaited, not just by those who adored it as a beverage and could also afford it, but also by people afflicted with every kind

of disease: it was indeed considered as a sort of panacea and the doctors of the time prescribed hot chocolate as a cure increasingly often.

The Germans were the last people to succumb to chocolate, but in the mid-17th century they too came under its spell, when Johann Georg Volkammer, a scholar from Nuremberg who had tasted it in Italy, returned to Germany singing the praises of chocolate.

A hundred years later, the first chocolate factory was opened in

prenez du Cacao
Van Houten

France, when M. de Pelletier founded the French Company of Chocolate and Tea in 1770.

Meanwhile, the cultivation of cocoa had also spread to Africa, especially on the high plateaus where the climate was extremely favourable. The yields were very high which was extremely satisfactory for the European colonists; indeed, production in Africa soon equalled that of America.

In the meantime, the first chocolate processing factories were set up in Switzerland. The very first was founded in Vevey in 1819 by M. Cailler who had previously worked in a chocolate factory in Turin, named after its founder, Caffarel, which is still in operation today. In 1824, the Suchard factory was set up in Neuchâtel, in the west of Switzerland, soon followed by Lindt and Tobler which are also all

still thriving in the world of chocolate today. It was Jean Tobler's experiments which led to the invention of milk chocolate, first launched on the market in 1870.

However, it was the Dutchman Van Houten who was responsible for producing the first soluble cocoa powder for drinking chocolate as it is known today, and which soon spread throughout Europe.

In Germany chocolate was considered a rarity, and its price, already high because of expensive transport costs, was made higher still by heavy taxation. The English discovered chocolate almost at the same time as the Germans, but at the start it appeared only as a whimsical frivolity in the rigid life of the aristocracy and rich upper classes. However, it soon caught on and consumption of chocolate quickly increased. In fact, a few years later, special establishments were set up where only drinking chocolate was served. These "exclusive" places were known as chocolate houses: the most famous ones were in London and were "White's" and "Cocoa Tree". They were visited by artists, writers, scholars and all who aspired to emulate the famous dandies of the English capital, at least in the eyes of the outside world.

In Switzerland, where chocolate had taken an unexpected importance, the success of the new drink was publicly acknowledged at a reception given by the mayor of Zurich, Heinrich Hescher who, on his return from Brussels, offered it to his friends to taste. In France too, drinking chocolate had become one of the "fashionable" drinks, so much so that by the time of Philip of Orléans an invitation to the "chocolate ceremony" was seen as a sign of great importance and acceptance by those who really counted. It was an invitation much sought-after by the aristocracy.

Chocolate in Italy

The first Italian to be interested in chocolate was a Milanese, Girolamo Bensoni, who tried to introduce it in Italy in 1556 after returning from France. However, it was the Florentine Francesco Carletti (1573-1636), a great traveller and merchant, who really introduced and converted the Italians to hot chocolate, the newly fashionable drink. Carletti had travelled to America after 1591 where he had visited the cocoa plantations. He immediately saw the vast potential of a well-organised cocoa trade and the enormous profits for anyone who took the initiative of bringing the dark beans that produced this delicious beverage to Europe. Carletti described cocoa as a plant which produces "such a famous

and important fruit" that in Bolivia and
Peru cocoa is consumed "worth over
five hundred thousand scudi every
year". Carletti further wrote that "this
fruit is also used as money to buy
small things at the market". He added
that "it is mainly used as a drink which
the Indians call 'chocolate', made by
mixing the fruit which are big like
acorns with hot water and sugar, having first dried them and roasted them
on the fire. They are ground on stones,
as we see painters do with their
colours, being rubbed for a long time

on a smooth flat, with a pestle, also made of stone. Thus a paste is formed which, when dissolved in water, becomes a beverage drunk by everyone in the country. And the Spanish and those of any other nation who have tasted it once, become so strongly addicted to it that they would find it extremely difficult to do without it every morning […]".

But cocoa was still far from being popular everywhere in Italy.

The first "industrial" chocolate factories in Italy were set up in Venice and Florence. Meanwhile in Rome in 1662, Cardinal Lorenzo Brancaccio discussed the possibility of drinking a cup of chocolate after Mass, as was traditional

among the ladies who had adopted this Spanish custom. The habit of drinking hot chocolate soon spread like wildfire among the clergy, and the liveried menservants arriving at the sacristy with cups of steaming chocolate were soon replaced by monks. In the dark, silent kitchens of the monasteries, those in charge of preparing hot chocolate soon became highly regarded. Wine had long been part of the church as a symbol of Christ's sacrifice, but now it was the turn of cocoa.

But unknown still was the secret of making the familiar chocolate bar of today, that indispensable booster of energy, and the source of such enjoyment to so many.

The first bar of chocolate was produced in England in 1820, thereby sparking off a fierce rivalry between the English and the natives of Turin as to the discovery of the techniques for solidifying chocolate. It seems that in 1802 a certain Signor Bozelli (who was actually of Genoese origin) had already experimented with a hydraulic machine designed to refine cocoa powder, which was then mixed with sugar, vanilla and hot water.

There is no doubt that Turin, the city where Bozelli worked, has a very long tradition of chocolate confectionery. This reputation is probably based on the large number of sophisticated confectioners there (and in the surrounding area such as None or Luserna San Giovanni) which still boast famous chocolate factories. The very names of Streglio, Baratti, Feletti, Peyrano and Croci rouse pleasant memories in the hearts of all who know Turin: coffee and pastries in the Corso Moncalieri, Via Cernaia, Piazza Castello, Via Mazzini, Corso Vittorio, Via

Avogadro, Piazza San Carlo, and many others...), confirming again that Turin is the capital of chocolate.

Turin is undoubtedly an elegant, sophisticated city, and it is generally agreed that chocolate – the Aztecs' "food of gods" – reveals a magical world of taste, fragrance and delicacy which finds its most perfect expression in delights such as the celebrated *gianduiotti*, nut chocolates of Piedmont.

Naturally, this supremacy is partly due to the craftsmanship and skill of the confectioners and the very high quality of the carefully selected raw materials. There are confectioners in Turin which boast over sixty kinds of chocolates. All have a delicious filling enclosed in luscious chocolate.

It is recommended that anyone who loves historical patisseries should go to the Piazza Castello: here, in the oldest patisserie of the city, Count Cavour who was particularly fond of *gianduiotti*, used to come and enjoy his favourite food.

Other confectioners specialised in producing very small chocolates or fresh cream puffs covered in chocolate. Yet others made stuffed panettone cake covered in thick chocolate, and pralines with a wide range of flavours.

Then a brilliant Bavarian pastry-maker called Pfatisch came to Turin.

He created amazing, incredibly refined chocolate tortas: the small chocolate meringue discs, the classic Montebianco torta, the Gianduia torta and the famous "salame nizzardo", which is a mixture of chocolate, cream, custard, rum, and biscotti, were all created bythis brilliant master of pastrymaking.

In fact, the Piedmontese tradition of chocolate goes back a very long way, given that Catherine of Austria, the daughter of Philip II of Spain and wife of Charles Emmanuel of Savoy was already a great consumer of chocolate.

After Spain, Italy was the country where chocolate was most popular in

Charles Emmanuel of Savoy and Catherine of Austria

Europe; while Piedmont, and Turin in particular, were the most important production centres and remained so throughout the 19th century until the beginning of the 20th century.

It was the master chocolate makers of Turin who developed the special chocolate paste known as *gianduia*, in honour of the popular mask of Turin, which combined chocolate paste with the finest Piedmontese hazelnuts. As often happens with gastronomic innovations as well as with important scientific discoveries and inventions, the "idea" of the *gianduia* was due to chance.

What happened was that because of the Napoleonic blockade, the Piedmontese chocolate makers were unable to obtain enough cocoa to serve their requirements. So they had the brilliant idea of making the cocoa go further by adding some locally-grown hazelnuts. This was particularly economical since there were no transport costs or shipping charges to pay.

The first *gianduiotto* was produced by Caffarel-Prochet in 1865, when the

PRIMA DEL PRANZO BEVETE L'AMARO SALUS
DOPO LA CREMA AL CIOCCOLATO GIANDUIA
LIQVORE GALLIANO

fears of the French naval blockade had already receded. At the time, it was given the name *givu* which means "a trifle" in the local dialect. The name *gianduia* and its legal registration took place in 1867. Today, more than a century later, the *gianduia* is still the same shape and size as the original chocolate.

Cocoa: a rich trade

America and Africa were now competing for supremacy in the cocoa trade. In fact, Africa has definitely overtaken America. Approximately 90 per cent of the cocoa on the market today is produced by eight African countries and seven American ones. All the cocoa producing countries are situated in the third world and experience serious economic problems. There are fifteen

TRAITÉS NOUVEAUX ET CURIEUX DU
CAFE DU THE, ET DU CHOCOLATE
Composée
Par Philippe Sylvestre Dufour.

major "consumer" countries which buy 85 per cent of the world production.

It is true that chocolate does not play as important a part as petrol in the world economic balance, but it is easy to see how even a small variation in the price of every sack of cocoa can mount up, so that enormous sums of money are involved. These changes are often not anticipated in the economic planning of the consumer countries. Variations in the price of cocoa are usually caused by exceptional weather conditions in the main producing countries (Brazil, Ivory Coast, Ghana, Nigeria and Cameroon). The price is also affected by the cost of fertilisers which are now increasingly used, as well as by damage caused by insects and fungal diseases.

Also, little is known with certainty about production data; this is often described as "incongruous". For instance, in the ten years between 1954 and 1963 it was stated that approximately 790,000 tons were produced per year, while in the next decade the annual average was 1,340,000 tons.

Because of these fluctuations, the organisations protecting the producers, recognising that prices are related directly to the quantities put on the market, have tried to counteract this by promoting the quality of the product.

In Ghana and Nigeria state monopolies share the financing and fix the

Americanus instructus suo vere Chocolaterio & Scypho — *pag. 141.*

Ramus arboris Cacao

...qua Fructus Cacao — *Fructus Cacao*

prices; in Brazil it is the State Department for Foreign Trade which establishes the standards of quality, and it supports the prices of those producers who observe these standards.

But this is all a matter of the internal organisation of the various producing countries. What is needed is a controlling organisation at an international level to regulate the cocoa trade. In

CONFETTERIA
BAR

CIOCCOLATO
BONATTI
LA GRAN MARCA
ITALIANA

SPECIALITA
BANANI

CIOCCOLATO
CREMA
CIOCCOLATO
SOVRANO
CIOCCOLATO
FORTUNE
CIRILLINO

*..... ricevdrem spuntate
il viaggiator tedesco a intedessate*

*c'assomolo lontan, che d'orà in poi
vogliamo fare e sappiom far dal noi*

1973 the International Cocoa Agreement was set up, but for a long time it was opposed by several economic organisations, especially the British who opposed "the imposition of restrictive systems which limited a free market".

In 1980 a new agreement was negotiated. The talks were held in London and they were neither peaceful nor easy, with the consumer countries being forced to accept the price offered by the producer countries of $1.20 per pound ($2.64 per kg), against the offer of $1.00 per pound ($2.20 per kg) by the consumer countries.

There was also an agreement based on the liquidation of funds at a set time in favour of the producer countries (about $220 million dollars were distributed to the producer countries).

The agreement contains precise, codified terms which are still in force today. These are the quality of the cocoa, the place of delivery, the date of delivery, and the conditions of delivery.

As far as the first condition is concerned, it is important to stress that the difference in price between the best quality ("fine" cocoa) and that defined as "ordinary" may be as much as 25 per cent. African producers are now planting new cultivars which may compete with the "fine", which typically is American cocoa (especially Brazilian).

The second condition requires that contracts must contain the phrase "CIF", meaning "carriage free to the destination port", or "FOB" which means "free on board" with all freight expenses, insurance and other costs born by the buyer.

The date of delivery must be given as a date within three months of the order. Deliveries are normally made in the months of May, June, July and December.

Purchase and preservation

In order to assess the price/quality ratio of chocolate properly – especially in view of the many types found on the market – it is always advisable to check the percentage of cocoa indicated on the package by the manufacturer. This is, after all, what determines the definition of the product. But how many qualities of chocolate are there?

The answer given by the producers is as follows: there is ordinary chocolate, chocolate, superior or very fine chocolate, and extra chocolate. But it is vital to check the percentage of cocoa in the preparation indicated on the package, because for instance some types of extra chocolate only contain 45 per cent, although there are others on the market with higher percentages, and therefore much more expensive.

It is of course also necessary to check the "sell by" date because, as every chocolate connoisseur knows, quality chocolate must break cleanly and melt on the tongue without becoming sticky. In addition, its surface must be completely smooth and solid.

To maintain chocolate in the best condition it is important to know that the packaging is capable of protecting it from light, humidity and air. This will help to preserve the characteristic aroma of the chocolate.

Chocolate should be stored in cool conditions, between 14 and 15°C (57 to 59°F), but not in a refrigerator because the humidity of the fridge could damage it and diminish the aroma. Milk chocolate should not be eaten more than a year after its production, while plain chocolate may be eaten up to 18 months from the date it was made.

GLOSSARY AND
SPECIAL PREPARATIONS

Glossary

Bain-marie: a method of cooking where moulds filled with a liquid to make puddings are immersed in a high-sided container, filled with very hot water. The mixture is then cooked further on a ring or in the oven until done.

Brioche pastry: light, soft yeast pastry made with flour, eggs, butter, milk and yeast, with or without sugar.

Charlotte: a thin sponge cake, shaped and cooked in the oven on a baking sheet, which can then be rolled to make pastries such as "logs" and so on.

Chocolate-flavoured custard sauce: confectioner's custard to which some drinking chocolate has been added with melted plain chocolate, diluted with a few drops of rum.

Coating: plain or milk chocolate which, after being melted in a bain-marie, can be used to make pralines or for glazing tortas, pastries, biscuits and the like.

Crème pâtissière (confectioner's custard): made from milk, eggs, flour and vanilla essence, well stirred using a wooden spoon. May be used in preparing chocolate-based puddings.

Gianduia cream: made by melting milk coating chocolate, mixing with hazelnut or almond purée, and adding maraschino or kirsch, and vanilla essence.

Gianduia pastry: soft pastry enriched with hazelnuts and chocolate, soaked in liqueur, filled with cream custard and chocolate, and coated with gelatine and chocolate.

Glazing or chocolate coating: coating torte or pastries with sugar, sauce, plain chocolate melted in a bain-marie, caramel and the like.

Madeleine pastry: light, sweet pastry, baked in the oven, also known as "Viennese pastry", made from flour, cornflour, eggs, butter and vanilla.

Used to make little cakes, puddings or as a base for tortas such as chocolate torta.

Prens: chocolate glaze used to cover torte, made by mixing pouring cream, caster sugar and glucose, to which the chocolate (broken into small pieces) is added when the mixture begins to boil.

Prens al rum: as above but with the addition of a few drops of Jamaica rum.

Ricotta pudding with chocolate: this is made by adding plain, unsweetened chocolate to ordinary ricotta. It is used with Sicilian cannoli.

Shortcrust pastry: pastry baked in the oven, made from flour, eggs, sugar, butter and salt; it may be flavoured with lemon zest or vanilla essence. Must be allowed to rest a few hours before using.

Whisking: the term used when a mixture with a buttery consistency must be made homogenous, but it also refers to straining and cooking a mixture to enhance the flavour and bind it better.

Coatings and chocolates

The so-called "coating chocolate" is chocolate which contains up to 40 per

cent cocoa butter, giving it sufficient fluidity to cover large surfaces with equal thickness.

It is a preparation which for a long time was produced by hand and used mostly by makers of pralines: roasted almonds, gianduia paste, marzipan or other confectionery, covered in sugar

and then in chocolate. It was also used by makers of chocolate Easter eggs, creams and pudding decorations.

In the past, coating chocolate was cooked in a saucepan in a bain-marie, but today there are thermostatically controlled pans which guarantee the right temperature for any operation.

The average temperature at which chocolate melts and reaches a perfectly smooth consistency is about 45° C (113° F). At this point it is important to keep stirring with a spatula because the chocolate tends to solidify very quickly. The mixture must be reheated slightly before dipping the fillings into the chocolate once it is fluid again.

When preparing chocolates filled with a crunchy centre, melt the milk coating chocolate with cocoa butter, then cut into squares (ovals or other shapes), going over them very lightly with a rolling pin to remove any imperfections, then cover them with plain chocolate by dipping them using a fork.

Making liqueur chocolates is far more complicated. Essential equipment includes a thermostatically controlled pan, wooden containers for starch, desiccated starch grains, a ruler to flatten the starch surface, a funnel for straining, a caramel thermometer, a copper container to cook the sugar, and a few rulers on which to stick the shapes or moulds.

The starch is placed in special containers; after 24 hours at about 38°C (100°F) the starch is shaken and levelled off in the containers with a ruler. The shapes of the chocolates are then pressed into the starch. The sugar is dissolved and cooked, then left to cool down. It is used to make a syrup from the liqueur, and then poured into the funnel which is used to fill the pre-moulded shapes in the starch very carefully. It is easy to see why this can only be done by professionals. But this does not mean that you should not try to make such chocolates at home!

First, melt some grated chocolate. Mix with peeled almonds (but this is not obligatory). Add the liqueur at this point and cook on a moderate heat; then remove from the heat and allow to set. Using your hands, shape into small balls or squares and roll them in coloured

Fürst von Metternich-Winneburg

sugar and bitter cocoa powder. The chocolates must now be put in the refrigerator for a few hours; one can also mix some pieces of candied fruit with the cocoa powder. This method is used to make the caramel or milk ganache, or chocolates filled with hazelnut praline, small caramel cups, orange-flavoured medallions, c*ervini*, *capricci* with marron glacé, doubloons, *tronchetti*, truffles, charlottes, *baci*, cream-filled chocolates and *boeri* (chocolates filled with liqueur and a cherry).

Sachertorte

In 1832 the Sachertorte was born. It happened almost by accident. Prince Metternich, Chancellor and Minister of Foreign Affairs to the Habsburg Emperor, Francis I, had asked his personal cook, Éduard Sacher, to prepare him a "solid, thick, virile" torta (Metternich was seventy years old). It seems that his cook made a mistake in the ingredients (eggs, butter, cocoa, apricot jam, sugar, flour, vanilla), and the result was the chocolate tart which became the jewel in the crown of Austrian cuisine which is still one of the most popular and successful Viennese pastries.

Bavarois

This is a pudding with a light, delicate consistency, based on thick egg custard and whipped cream, and gelatine. It may be flavoured with jam, chocolate, vanilla and other fragrances, with candied or fresh fruit. The mixture is poured into a special low-sided mould in which it is left to cool down. To make chocolate bavarois, add 120 g of grated plain chocolate to egg yolks and sweetened milk.

Easter eggs

These have always been very popular everywhere. Naturally, to make chocolate eggs the appropriate moulds are needed; when these were still produced by craftsmen, before the industrial production of the present day, they were made of metal and are now sought-after. Today they are made of food-grade plastic.

Whether metal or plastic, the moulds are eggshell halves in the required size, used several times to make what could be called the "batch". The part which is in contact with the chocolate must be very clean. The chocolate is dissolved using the old method of a saucepan in a bain-marie. The mixture is then allowed to thicken before being put into the moulds, making sure that the excess mixture is removed when the mould is placed upside down on a wire grill. It is up to the person making the chocolate eggs to decide how long the chocolate must remain in the mould to obtain the right

thickness, a fact which will be reflected in the selling price.

To join the two halves, a little melted chocolate is placed along the edge of one of the halves which is then lightly pressed against the other, while trying to avoid dripping or irregularities.

Today, chocolate eggs are made quite differently, both to avoid the fragility of the chocolate shell and the excessive thickness which would raise the price: the chocolate mixture is put into the moulds using an instrument known as a "flat brush", which is dipped in the melted chocolate and spread on the sides of the mould. The moulds are then left to cool down in the fridge.

But why is it that eggs are eaten at Easter time? The reason is that since time immemorial the egg has been considered auspicious in every civilisation: it was considered a symbol of life in Egypt, the fertility of the earth in Greece, and the quintessence of life for the Phoenicians.

In Christianity eggs were blessed, and in the 15th century eggs became an Easter offering. But when cocoa was discovered, the egg became ... a chocolate egg, usually with a "surprise" inside it.

Cocoa and its derivatives according to the law

Cocoa powder: this is obtained by grinding cocoa beans and it must contain at least 20 per cent cocoa butter.

Extra plain chocolate: this contains at least 45 per cent cocoa.

Gianduia chocolate: this is made from chocolate (containing at least 32 per cent cocoa) and ground hazelnuts (20–40 g for each 100 g of the product) and sometimes also pieces of almonds, hazelnuts or nuts.

Light cocoa powder: this contains at least 1.8 per cent cocoa butter.

Milk chocolate: milk or dehydrated milk products are added, sometimes with cream, butter or butter fats. It must contain at least 25 per cent cocoa, 14 per cent milk products and 3.5 per cent butter fats. The saccharose must not exceed 55 per cent.

Ordinary chocolate: this is made from cocoa paste, cocoa powder or cocoa granules, saccharose and sometimes cocoa butter. It must contain at least 30 per cent cocoa butter.

Soluble cocoa: cocoa powder which has undergone carbonated steam treatment.

Superior or very fine plain chocolate: this contains at least 43 per cent cocoa.

Superior or very fine milk chocolate: this contains at least 30 per cent cocoa,

18 per cent milk-based products and 4.5 per cent butterfat.

Sweetened cocoa powder: cocoa powder mixed with saccharose and containing at least 32 per cent cocoa.

White chocolate: a mixture of saccharose (no more than 55 per cent), cocoa butter (at least 20 per cent), milk or dehydrated milk derivatives (at least 14 per cent) and sometimes also cream. Colouring agents are always strictly forbidden.

RECIPES

NB: The amounts given here are intended for four people, except where otherwise indicated

BASIC PREPARATIONS

Here are the recipes for a few standard basic preparations which are included in many of the recipes.

Sponge cake. Ingredients: 5 eggs; 150 g caster sugar; 125 g flour; 20 g butter. Whisk the egg yolks in a bowl with the sugar until the mixture is a very pale yellow. Then add the flour and melted butter. Beat the egg whites until stiff and fold in very carefully into the mixture. Put the resulting mixture in a round cake tin and bake in an oven pre-heated to 200° C (400° F) for approximately 30 minutes. Depending on the kind of pudding it is to be used in, square or rectangular tins may also be used. Cooking times may also vary depending on the recipe.

Chocolate sponge: The method and ingredients are the same as those for traditional sponge, but when adding the flour, 30 g of plain cocoa powder is added as well.

Chocolate custard. Ingredients: 250 g whipping cream; 300 g plain chocolate. Put the cream in a saucepan, bring to the boil and cook for one minute. Remove from the heat and pour on the chocolate which has first been broken into pieces. Stir with a fine whisk until the mixture is smooth and homogenous. Allow to cool down at room temperature. There is also a coffee variation of this recipe using coffee-flavoured chocolate instead of plain chocolate. There is also the Regina version which uses chocolate with hazelnuts in addition to plain chocolate, following the proportions indicated in the individual recipes.

Confectioner's custard or crème pâtissière. Ingredients: 3 tablespoons sugar, 3 egg yolks; 3 tablespoons flour, ½ litre milk, zest of a lemon.

Stir the sugar into the egg yolks until smooth, then sprinkle the flour into the mixture. Heat the milk and when it has almost reached boiling point, pour in a little at a time into the mixture, stirring well to avoid any lumps. Bring to the boil on a very low heat and simmer for a few minutes while stirring continuously. Remove the custard from the heat, add the lemon zest and allow to cool down a bit.

Chocolate and custard ring

Ingredients: 50 g plain chocolate; 180 g butter; 180 g sugar; 3 eggs, 250 g white flour; yeast for puddings; 1 glass milk; pinch of salt.

Melt the chocolate in a little of the butter and allow to cool down. In another bowl, whisk the remaining butter with the sugar. Add the eggs, flour, yeast and salt and mix together. Stir in the milk, continuing to stir until all the mixture is homogenous and smooth, then divide into two portions and add the cooled-down chocolate to one of the portions. Butter a ring-shaped mould, sprinkle with flour and arrange the components in layers in the mould. Bake in the oven at 180° C (350° F) for about an hour.

Chocolate and coffee ice cream

Ingredients: 60 g plain chocolate; 2 tablespoons water, 180 g whipping cream; 130 g caster sugar; 200 ml coffee. Break the chocolate into pieces and put in the saucepan. Add the water and heat gently to melt the chocolate, stirring all the time. Allow to cool down, then add the cream, sugar and coffee. Pour into an ice-cream machine and leave to be stirred for half an hour.

Orange-flavoured chocolate "tego-line" (chocolate almond biscuits)

Ingredients: 8 oranges; 300 g caster sugar; 6 eggs; 4 sheets of gelatine; 2 tablespoons brandy; ¼ litre cream; 4 chocolate tegoline.

Finely chop the peel of three of the oranges and sprinkle with sugar. Whisk the egg yolks with about 125 g of the sugar, adding the gelatine which has been dissolved in the hot brandy. Heat up 100 g of the sugar in a little water in a pan to make a syrup. Beat the egg whites until stiff and add the sugar syrup while still hot. Add the beaten egg yolks, the chopped peel, the juice of the three oranges and the whipped cream. Pour the resulting mousse into a mould and leave in the fridge for at least three hours. Squeeze the remaining oranges, finely slice the peel of two oranges, and add the juice and peel to the rest of the sugar. Bring to the boil and simmer until the mixture turns into a thick syrup which is then left to cool down. Shape the mousse into balls and arrange at the centre of the chocolate tegoline. Serve with the orange sauce.

Chocolate figs

Ingredients: 400 g dried figs;
120 g roasted almonds; 80 g chopped
candied citron-peel; 2 chopped cloves;
80 g cocoa (you can also use similar
amountsof grated plain chocolate);
80 g icing sugar.

Cut the figs half open and stuff each with an almond and a few pieces of chopped candied citron-peel and cloves. Carefully close the figs again, place them on a baking sheet and bake for about 15 minutes in the oven at 160° C (320° F) until they begin to turn golden. Remove them from the baking sheet and roll them, still hot, in a mixture of the cocoa powder and sugar, or dip them in chocolate melted in a saucepan with a little water and icing sugar. These figs can be kept for a long time in a wooden box or tin.

Torta Sylvie
Ingredients (for 8 people): 400 g plain
chocolate; 3–4 tablespoons milk; 200 g
butter; 200 g sugar; 8 eggs; 100 g flour.

Melt the chocolate in the milk in a saucepan, stirring well using a wooden spoon. Melt the butter in a saucepan on a low heat and add to the melted chocolate. Beat all the egg yolks and sugar vigorously in a bowl, then fold in the flour and finally the melted chocolate, stirring all the while. Beat the egg whites until they stand in stiff peaks and carefully fold into the mixture. Pour this mixture into a hinged cake-tin 26 cm (10 in) in diameter, lined with greaseproof paper. Bake for about 50 minutes in an oven pre-heated to 200° C (400° F). Allow to cool down and remove the cake from the tin. It is delicious with whipped cream.

Chocolate torta with cinnamon and fennel

Ingredients: 250 g shortcrust pastry; 250 g brioche pastry; 150 g butter; 150 g icing sugar; 4 egg yolks; 50 g flour type 0; 100 g cocoa powder; 100 g chopped almonds; a pinch of cinnamon;

a pinch of fennel; 4 beaten egg whites;
maraschino syrup (optional).

Work the shortcrust pastry and brioche dough together; put in a cake tin. Cream the butter and sugar, add the egg yolks one by one, then the flour, cocoa powder, chopped almonds, cinnamon, fennel and beaten egg whites. Put the cake tin in the oven and bake in the oven at approximately 180° C (350° F) for at least 35 minutes, or until it has turned golden. It can be served with maraschino syrup which further enhances the taste.

Almond pudding

Ingredients (for 8 people): 6 egg whites;
180 g peeled almonds; 180 g sugar;
chocolate custard (prepared according
to the method and amounts indicated);
a little cocoa powder for dusting.

Beat the egg whites until stiff. Chop the almonds together with the sugar in a blender and carefully fold into the egg whites. Butter and sprinkle a cake tin with a little flour. Using a pastry bag, make two circles with the egg white mixture, approximately 20 cm in diameter. Bake for about 8 minutes in an oven preheated to approximately 230° C (450° F), then allow to cool down. Make the chocolate custard and cover one circle with it. Place the other circle on top and cover with the remaining chocolate custard. Sprinkle with cocoa powder and serve immediately, or store in the fridge for up to 24 hours.

Chocolate mousse

Ingredients (for 6 people): 350 g plain chocolate; 2 or 3 tablespooons milk; 30 g butter; 6 eggs; 100 g icing sugar.
Melt the chocolate in the milk in a bain-marie. Stir with a wooden spoon until the mixture is completely smooth. Melt the butter and add to the chocolate. In a bowl, beat the egg yolks and sugar, add the lukewarm chocolate and stir well. Beat the egg whites until they form stiff peaks and carefully fold into

the chocolate mixture. Now carefully spoon the resulting mixture into a glass dish or individual bowls and leave to cool down in the fridge for an hour.

This delicious mousse can be served with whipped cream or biscuits such as "langue de chat".

Chocolate soufflé

Ingredients (for 5 people): 40 g butter; 30 g flour; 6 eggs; 100 g icing sugar; 200 g plain chocolate; 2–3 tablespoons milk.
Melt the butter and add the flour, using a wooden spoon to stir the mixture until smooth. Beat the egg yolks and the sugar until creamy and pale. Beat the egg whites until they form stiff peaks. Melt the chocolate in the milk and stir into the egg and butter mixture. Add the beaten egg whites. Pour the resulting mixture into a well buttered soufflé dish and bake for about 40 minutes in an oven preheated to 200° C (400° F). When the soufflé has risen sufficiently, remove from the oven and serve immediately.

Poires belle Hélène

*Ingredients (for 6–8 people): 400 g
sugar; ½ vanilla stick; 8 pears
(Williams); 500 g fresh cream; 130 g
plain chocolate, vanilla ice cream.*

In a saucepan, make a syrup by boiling
1 litre of water with the sugar and the
vanilla. Peel the pears, remove the
cores and cut into halves. Put the pear
halves into the syrup and simmer on a
very low heat for about 5–10 minutes.
Remove the pears from the syrup and
drain. Make a chocolate sauce by boiling the fresh cream for 2 minutes, then
adding the chocolate broken into small
pieces. Stir the mixture with a wooden
spoon until the chocolate has melted
completely and the mixture is smooth.
Arrange the pears in a dish or if pre-
ferred in individual bowls. Add a
spoonful of vanilla ice cream onto each
pear and pour the hot chocolate sauce
on top. Serve immediately.

Rice pudding with cocoa

Ingredients (for 6 people): 1 litre milk; 200 g rice; 50 g butter; 200 g caster sugar; 70 g plain cocoa powder; orange zest; 20 g sultanas (soaked); 4 eggs.

Put the milk in a saucepan and when it is about to boil, add the rice and butter. Bring to the boil and simmer on a low heat for about 50 minutes. As soon as the rice is cooked, add the sugar, the plain cocoa powder, the orange zest and the sultanas, previously soaked in lukewarm water. Mix well. When the mixture has cooled down, add the egg yolks and carefully fold in the beaten egg whites. Spoon the mixture into a buttered mould and bake for about 35 minutes in an oven preheated to approximately 180° C (350° F). Serve lukewarm.

Chocolate Charlotte

Ingredients (for 6 people): 130 g caster sugar; 4 tablespoons kirsch liqueur; 6 eggs; 250 g plain chocolate; 30 g butter; sponge fingers (about 25).

In a saucepan melt 100g of the sugar with approximately 200 ml water. Allow to cool down and add the kirsch. Whisk together the egg yolks and remaining sugar and beat the egg whites until they stand in stiff peaks. Melt the chocolate in a bain-marie, and when it has melted and the mixture is completely smooth, add the egg yolks and the softened butter. Add the beaten egg whites to this mixture, folding them in very carefully. Pour the melted sugar with the kirsch into a bowl and put the sponge fingers in, one by one. Line the bowl with the biscuits soaked in the kirsch and melted sugar, lining the bottom first, then arranging them vertically side by side round the bowl. Pour the chocolate into the bowl and cover with more biscuits soaked in kirsch. Leave the pudding in the refrigerator for at least 12 hours, Turn out on a serving dish and serve immediately.

Chocolate pudding with chestnuts

Ingredients (for 6 people): 200 g plain chocolate; 400 g chestnut purée;

sponge cake (made according to the method and in the proportions indicated); 100 ml fresh whipping cream; 240 g caster sugar; 2 egg whites; 2 tablespoons rum.

Beat the egg whites until they stand in stiff peaks with 40 g of the sugar. When the egg whites are nearly stiff, add the remaining 80 g of the sugar. Bake the egg whites, shaped into circles, on a baking sheet lined with greaseproof paper at a temperature of 60° C (140° F) for about 50 minutes. Make a syrup by melting the remaining sugar with 3 or 4 tablespoons of water in a saucepan. Bring it to the boil stirring all the while. Then remove it from the heat and add the rum. Pour the cream into a saucepan and bring to the boil. Remove from the heat and add the chocolate, broken into pieces. Stir well until the chocolate has melted completely and the mixture is smooth. Cut the sponge cake in two horizontally. Place the first half on a serving dish, coat with a layer of the syrup and spread about a quarter of the chocolate sauce on top. Now add a layer of chestnut purée and then, in the following order, the meringue circle, another quarter of the chocolate sauce, the other half of the chestnut puree and finally the other sponge cake half, coated with syrup. Cover the entire pudding with the rest of the chocolate sauce and refrigerate for 3 hours.

The lady's secret

Ingredients (for 4 people): 1 egg;
1 egg yolk; 130 g caster sugar;
80 g plain cocoa powder; 75 g butter;
50 g hazelnuts; 100g dry biscuits.

Put the whole egg, egg yolk and sugar in a bowl and whisk well to obtain a smooth, creamy mixture. Add the cocoa powder and stir well to make sure it is well incorporated. Now add the softened butter, stirring all the while. Chop the hazelnuts and crumble the biscuits into not-too-small pieces: Add both to the mixture and stir again. Pour carefully into a cake tin lined with cling film and put in the refrigerator for at least half an hour. Take the pudding out of the fridge, remove from the mould and cut into slices.

Mascarpone and chocolate pudding

Ingredients (for 6 people): 4 eggs; 4 soupspoons caster sugar; ½ kg mascarpone; 100 g plain chocolate; 100 g sponge fingers soaked in cup of strong black coffee; cocoa powder for dusting.

In a bowl, whisk together the egg yolks with the sugar until the mixture becomes creamy. Fold in the mascarpone and stir until you obtain a smooth consistency. In a saucepan, melt the chocolate in a little milk, allow to cool down and add to the mixture. Beat the egg whites until they stand in very firm peaks and fold carefully into the mixture. In a high-sided bowl, start with a layer of the creamy mixture, then arrange a layer of the sponge fingers soaked in coffee. Add another layer of the creamy mixture, then another layer of sponge fingers. Cover the whole with a third layer of creamy mixture and sprinkle with plain cocoa powder. Put in the fridge for an hour. Serve the pudding chilled but not too cold.

Chocolate truffles

Ingredients: 130 g water; 60 g butter; 80 g flour; 2 eggs; chocolate custard (made following the method and in the proportions indicated); plain cocoa powder.

First of all, prepare the paste for the truffles. In a saucepan, put the water with the butter and a pinch of salt. Bring to the boil. When the water begins to boil, remove from the heat and add the flour. Return the pan to the heat, stirring until the flour comes off the sides of the pan, forming a ball. Allow to cool down and add the eggs until the mixture is smooth and homogeneous.

Put the dough in a pastry bag and – on a buttered baking-sheet – make balls the size of large walnuts. Cook the truffles in the oven for 10 minutes at 200° C (400° F) and let them cool down. Fill them with the chocolate custard, and also cover them in the custard, finally rolling them in the plain cocoa powder to give them their characteristic truffle appearance.

Chocolate cloud

Ingredients (for 4 people): 70 g butter; 100 g flour; ½ litre warm milk; 50 g plain cocoa powder; 180 g sugar; 4 eggs.

In a saucepan, melt the butter and add the flour and the milk, stirring all the while. Bring to the boil and allow to simmer for a few minutes until the mixture thickens. Remove from the heat and add the plain cocoa powder and sugar. When the mixture has cooled down, add the egg yolks, then the beaten egg whites. Put the resulting mixture in a soufflé dish and bake for 30 minutes at 180° C (350° F). Serve as soon as it has risen.

Chocolate strudel

Ingredients (for 4 people): 4 apples; 4 pears; grated rind of a lemon; 80 g sultanas (softened in lukewarm water); 50 g pine kernels; 4 tablespoons fig jam; 200 g plain chocolate; 250 g puff pastry.

In a bowl, finely slice the apples and pears, then add the grated lemon rind and the sultanas. Add the pine kernels and fig jam, and stir well. In a saucepan, melt the chocolate, and when it has cooled down a little, add half the fruit to it. Put the puff pastry, shaped into a rectangle, on a baking sheet lined with greaseproof paper. Pour the fruit mixture on it, then roll the pastry and close the edges carefully. Brush the strudel with some beaten egg and bake in the oven for about 40 minutes at 180° C (350° F). Serve the strudel lukewarm with the remaining melted chocolate.

Guinea fowl with chocolate

Ingredients (for 4 people): a guinea fowl of about 1.5 kg; 3 spoonfuls plain cocoa powder; 50 g butter; 2 tablespoons olive oil; 50 g bacon slices; parsley; 4 small white onions; 3 sticks celery; 10 carrots; 1 bottle dry sparkling white wine; 50 g single cream.
Clean the guinea fowl thoroughly, then season with salt and pepper, and put the cocoa powder inside the bird. In a

saucepan, heat the butter and the oil, and add the bacon. Put the guinea fowl in the saucepan and cook on a high heat until brown. Now reduce the heat to medium and add the parsley, onions, celery, and carrots cut into small pieces. Cook for 10 minutes. Pour the whole bottle of sparkling wine into the pan, cover and cook on a high heat until the sauce has reduced to at least a third. Reduce the heat again and cook for another 40 minutes. Remove the guinea fowl from the casserole, cut it into pieces and arrange on a serving dish. Put all the vegetables through the blender. Return them to the casserole, and add the cream. Season the sauce with salt and pepper. When very hot pour it onto the guinea fowl pieces and serve immediately.

Hare in chocolate orange sauce

Ingredients (for 4 people): 1 small white onion; 2 sticks celery; 2 carrots; 2 tablespoons vegetable oil;

40 g prosciutto crudo; 1 hare weighing about 2 kg; 150 ml hot meat stock; 50 g sultanas (softened in lukewarm water);40 g pine kernels; 30 g candied orange; 40 g plain chocolate; 40 g caster sugar; ¼ glass wine vinegar.

Mix the onion, celery and carrots together and cook with the prosciutto in oil in a saucepan until the vegetables are soft. Add the cleaned hare cut into small pieces. Fry until brown on a high heat, then reduce the heat and continue to cook, adding some of the stock now and again to keep it moist. Put the sultanas, the pine kernels, candied orange, chocolate, sugar and the vinegar in a bowl. Pour this mixture over the hare and allow to boil for a few more minutes in order to ensure that the sauce is well amalgamated. Arrange the hare pieces on a serving dish and serve hot.

Bibliography

Bernal Díaz del Castillo, *Storia della conquista del Messico*, n.d.

Hernán Cortés, *Lettere a Carlo V*, n.d.

Corporazione dei Pasticceri, *Das Goldene Kochbuch*, Steiemark, n.d.

A. Brillat Savarin, *Anathomie du goût*, Paris, 1825.

Mario Spagnoli, *La fabbricazione del cioccolato*, Milan, 1926.

Various authors, *Il cioccolato e il suo valore alimentare*, Feder. Industrie Dolciarie, no. 20, 1933.

Pierre Andrieu, *La grande cucina francese*, Bologna, 1964.

Alberto Lodispoto, *Enciclopedia dell'Alimentazione*, Saluzzo, 1972.

Giuseppe Dematteis, *Viaggio in Italia: Torino*, Milan, 1982.

Various authors, *Grande Enciclopedia illustrata della Gastronomia*, Milan, 1990.

E. Casati, G. Ortona, *Il cioccolato*, Bologna, 1990.

INDEX

ACKNOWLEDGEMENTS

The author thanks Nestlé Italiana s.p.a. for the wealth of information provided. Thanks also to Marina Dini for essential help in writing the recipes.

The Connoisseur's Companions
Also in the series:

Coffee
A vast expanse of information about the timeless beverage that is coffee; a compact guide to a complex ingredient.

Whisky
An intriguing account that explains why whisky has become one of the most important drinks in the world. No whisky devotee will want to be without this book.

Olive Oil
Olive oil has become the single most important ingredient in cooking today. Also featuring delicious recipes, this is a useful, concise, easy-to-follow guide.